Judges 9-21

LEARNING TO LIVE GOD'S WAY

CWR

Phin Hall

Copyright © CWR 2013

Published 2013 by CWR, Waverley Abbey House, Waverley Lane, Farnham, Surrey GU9 8EP, UK. CWR is a Registered Charity – Number 294387 and a Limited Company registered in England – Registration Number 1990308.

The right of Phin Hall to be identified as the author of this work has been asserted by him in accordance with the Copyright, Designs and Patents Act 1988, sections 77 and 78.

All rights reserved. No part of this publication may be reproduced, stored in a retrieval system, or transmitted, in any form or by any means, electronic, mechanical, photocopying, recording or otherwise, without the prior permission in writing of CWR.

See back of book for list of National Distributors.

Unless otherwise indicated, all Scripture references are from the Holy Bible: New International Version (Anglicised edition), copyright © 1979, 1984, 2011 by Biblica (formally International Bible Society).

Concept development, editing, design and production by CWR.

Printed in the UK by Page Brothers.

ISBN: 978-1-85345-910-8

Contents

4   Introduction

7   Week 1
Abimelech: The Man who would be King
Judges 9:1-10:5

13   Week 2
The Vow, the Victory and the Virgin
Judges 10:6-12:15

19   Week 3
Samson's Great Strength
Judges 13:1-15:20

25   Week 4
Samson's Great Weakness
Judges 16

31   Week 5
The Trouble with Idols
Judges 17:1-18:31

37   Week 6
The Best Will in the World
Judges 19:1-20:48

43   Week 7
Marriage Vows
Judges 21

49   Leader's Notes

Introduction

'Oh no, not Judges again! Why is this book even in the Bible?'

This was one of the comments that greeted the news that our Bible study group would be continuing our journey through the book of Judges. Just when you thought it was safe to get back into the Old Testament … thousands of men, women and children are slaughtered, and hundreds of women are raped, including one whose body is then cut up and mailed around the countryside. Even in the opening session, seventy men are sacrificed in a single day by their own half-brother! It is almost as if the narrator is deliberately trying to shock us with the most negative accounts about Israel that he can find. But why would he do that?

The book of Judges covers a period of around 300 years from the end of Joshua's leadership to the birth of Samuel. In this study guide we join the narrative over 200 years into this period. Four of the major judges have already been and gone: the exemplary Othniel, the cunning Ehud, the trio of Deborah, Barak and Jael, and the capricious Gideon. The accounts of their leadership revealed much about the nature of faith – what it is, how it is demonstrated through our lives, how God shapes and grows our faith, how important it is, and how much can be achieved when, in faith, we work together with God. Now only two major judges remain.

The title, 'judge', does not really do justice to the role these people played – they did not wear wigs and robes or hang out in courtrooms. A more accurate title might be 'saviour', 'deliverer', or even 'warlord', since the main task of the judges was to go to war against the nations who oppressed Israel. And this happened a lot, thanks to the cycle of events in which the Israelites kept getting caught.

Introduction

This cycle is described in the second chapter of Judges, and followed this pattern:
- The Israelites worshipped idols instead of God;
- God allowed a foreign nation to oppress them;
- They cried out to God, who raised up a judge to deliver them;
- The Israelites worshipped idols instead of God ... and so on.

Six accounts of this cycle are given in Judges, and far from learning their lesson, the Israelites get progressively worse as the cycles unfold. The book of Judges is, therefore, more an account of Israel's downward spiral than simply a repeated cycle of events.

As if that was not gloomy enough, Judges closes with two epilogues, both dating from early in this period. The first gives an example of the ease with which God's people turned to idols even while they thought they were serving God, and the second gives an incredibly gruesome example of how rash and violent they were. A lot of people die!

So, faced with the gory details, the downward spiral of Israel and the prospect of an unhappy ending, the question of why Judges is even in the Bible – and why the narrator would choose to portray the nation so negatively – remains.

In 1 Corinthians 10, Paul gives us our reason. Writing about the troubled times of Israel's past, he says, 'These things happened to them as examples and were written down as warnings for us, on whom the fulfilment of the ages has come' (v.11). Even in the midst of the horror and the humiliation, God is speaking to us through His Word, teaching us and warning us. And sometimes the most negative examples give us the most positive instruction.

The epilogue opens and closes with the statement that 'everyone did as he saw fit' (Judg. 17:6; 21:25). Here then we have the heart of what these closing chapters of Judges have to teach us; they teach us that God's ways are the best:
- His justice is best, because He sees all outcomes.
- His promises are best, because only He has the power to fulfil them.
- His plans are best, because they work for His glory and our good.
- His desires are best, because He alone is good.
- His opinion is best, because He cannot be swayed by the expectation of others.
- His will is best, because what is right in His eyes is pure and perfect – God has no mixed motives!

In addition to this, our journey through these closing chapters also calls us to consider the importance of Bible knowledge and of recognising the voice of the Holy Spirit and following His guidance. When you think of all it has in store for us, surely even the book of Judges, whose inclusion in Scripture we may at times question, is worth our time and attention!

You will get the most out of these sessions if you take the time to read through the complete passage assigned to each one before you start working through the Discussion Starters. Some of these passages are fairly long, but be encouraged, they really are worth the effort.

Our prayer is that, as you use this study guide, and work your way through these final, thrilling chapters of Judges, you will grow in your awe and delight in God and in His ways which really are the best!

WEEK | ONE

WEEK 1

Abimelech:
The Man who would be King

Opening Icebreaker

In 2011 a convicted kidnapper sued his hostages for breach of contract, because they told the police where he was hiding when they had promised not to! Share other lawsuits you believe are outrageous that you have heard of.

Bible Readings

- Judges 9:1–10:5
  (if short of time just read Judges 9:1–21 and 42–57)
- Psalm 135:6
- Romans 8:28
- Romans 12:19
- 1 Peter 2:23

Key Verse: 'Thus God repaid the wickedness that Abimelech had done to his father by murdering his seventy brothers.' (9:56)

Focus: We all long for justice, but God's justice is best.

Judges 9-21

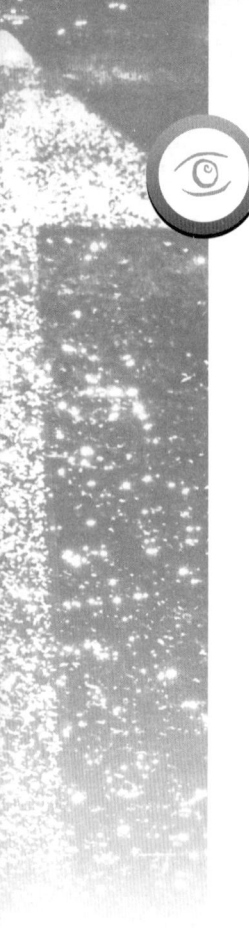

Opening Our Eyes

Abimelech was neither a true Israelite nor a true heir of Gideon. He was the son of Gideon's concubine from Shechem and as such he had none of the rights of his seventy half-brothers, all of whom *were* Israelites. Even his own name (meaning 'my father is king') would have been a constant reminder that he was denied a share in Gideon's glory. The injustice of his situation seems to have fuelled an insatiable desire for revenge, and so Judges 9 opens with Abimelech making his move to seize power.

He began by winning over the people of Shechem, calling on them to reject the rulership of Gideon's other sons in his favour. They agreed to make him king, giving him silver to hire an army of 'reckless scoundrels'.

The brutal massacre of Gideon's seventy sons is summed up in a single sentence in verse 5, but the phrase 'on one stone' effectively communicates the horror of this event. One can imagine only too easily this crowd of young men being slaughtered one after another, like animals on an altar, their bodies piling up and the ground soaked with their blood.

Having dealt with his rivals, Abimelech was crowned at Shechem, one of Israel's key spiritual landmarks. Here, God had first promised the land to Abraham, the bones of Joseph had been laid to rest, and Joshua had called on the Israelites to serve the Lord. Now their first king was crowned here – an outsider who had slaughtered his own brothers in his thirst for vengeance and power!

It is worth noting that God is never mentioned in this account by His covenant name 'Yahweh' (or 'Lord'). This emphasises the point made at the end of Judges 8, that the Israelites 'did not remember the Lord their God, who had rescued them from the hands of all their enemies on every side' (8:34). However, this does not mean that God was uninterested. On the contrary, we can clearly see Him at work as Jotham, Gideon's sole surviving son, returned to speak at Abimelech's coronation. His speech begins with a parable in which the trees search for a king, with the clear implication that Abimelech is a fruitless, inadequate choice of king.

It is followed by a curse: '... let fire come out from Abimelech and consume you, the citizens of Shechem and Beth Millo, and let fire come out from you ... and consume Abimelech!' (9:20). As events unfold, we see this was not simply Jotham's anger that was speaking, but God's justice, which would soon be set in motion.

Three years later, 'God sent an evil spirit between Abimelech and the citizens of Shechem' (9:23). It began with the visit of a man called Gaal, who, using the same tactics as Abimelech, gained the favour and support of Shechem. Informed of this treachery, Abimelech acted swiftly, driving out the usurper and killing many of his men.

However, Abimelech's desire for revenge was not so easily satisfied. Next he destroyed Shechem, burning down the temple where the townsfolk had hidden. Even this did not satisfy Abimelech, who went on to attack the nearby city of Thebez, seemingly unprovoked. Finally, the trail of death and destruction was brought to an end as one of the women hiding in the tower there dropped a millstone onto Abimelech's head, crushing his skull.

And so Jotham's words were fulfilled – the people of Shechem and the evil king Abimelech had destroyed each other. God's justice had repaid them for their wickedness.

Judges 9-21

 **Discussion Starters**

1. What was most striking for you in this account?

2. Why do you think Abimelech slaughtered Gideon's other sons, together with the people of Shechem, in such a brutal fashion?

3. Abimelech's downfall came as he sought justice for the treachery of Shechem. However, this seems more like a desire for revenge than justice as does the murder of his brothers. What is the difference between revenge and justice?

4. Consider times when you have been frustrated by injustice, whether against yourself or others. Is it always justice you desire or is it also sometimes revenge?

Abimelech: The Man who would be King

5. Read Psalm 135:6, Romans 8:28 and 1 Peter 2:23. While God is not mentioned by His covenant name in the account of Abimelech in Judges 9, verses 23–24 and 56–57 give us insight into what was occurring behind the scenes. How does this affect your understanding of God's justice?

6. Read Romans 12:19. How is it possible to trust that God's justice is best at times when you want revenge?

7. How would you answer a non-Christian who asks, 'How can you say God is just when there is so much suffering in the world and yet many bad people live their lives in luxury?'

Judges 9-21

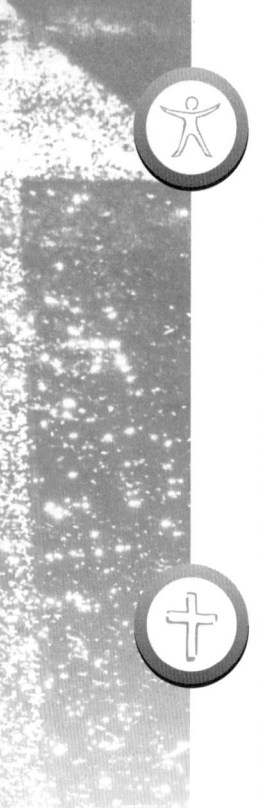

Personal Application

All of us will have longed for justice at some time, whether for wrongs done to others or to ourselves. Even children seem to have an inbuilt sense of justice, and are very quick to point out when something is unfair! One of the most common attacks on Christianity is that so often justice seems to be left undone.

However, none of us can see the whole picture, and know when justice is *really* done. God alone sees all things, from the biggest action to the smallest incident, and so He alone is in a position to judge justly. But can we really trust that His justice is best?

Seeing Jesus in the Scriptures

The great defence we have, when people point out the injustice that seems prevalent all around us, is the knowledge that a day is coming when absolute justice will be done. Every person who has ever lived will stand and be judged.

But before whom will they stand? Who will be the judge? None other than Jesus – He who suffered the ultimate injustice. To save His people and bring them back to Himself, God came to earth. He lived among those He created, sustained and loved, yet He was despised and rejected, ridiculed and executed.

However, a day is coming when 'Christ Jesus … will judge the living and the dead …' (2 Tim. 4:1). On that day, every thought, every word, every deed, every accident, every incident, every natural disaster will be dealt with for all to see. Jesus will ensure that justice is done!

WEEK 2

The Vow, the Victory and the Virgin

Opening Icebreaker

Sitting in a circle, one person has an object such as a small beanbag. They throw this to another member of the group, saying 'catch' or 'drop' as they do so. The person to whom the object is thrown has to do the opposite of what the thrower said (ie drop it if they said 'catch'). If they do this correctly, they then become the thrower. If they fail, they are 'out' and the object is passed back to the thrower. The game continues until only one person is 'in'.

Bible Readings

- Judges 10:6–12:15 (if short of time just read 11:1–12, 29–40)
- Psalm 145:8
- 1 Corinthians 13:4
- Proverbs 14:30
- James 5:10–12
- Ecclesiastes 5:2–5

Key Verse: 'Oh! My daughter! You have made me miserable and wretched, because I have made a vow to the LORD that I cannot break.' (11:35)

Focus: At times we all make promises, but God's promises are best.

Judges 9-21

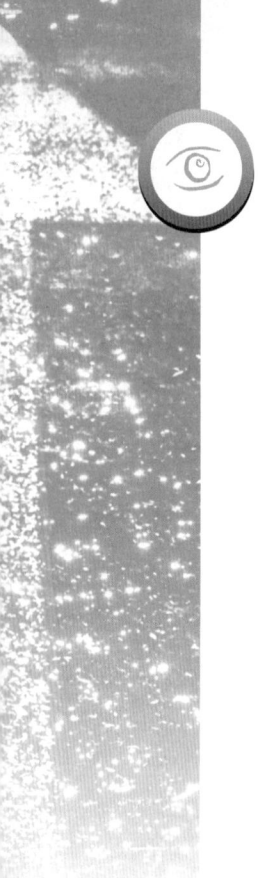 **Opening Our Eyes**

The cycle of Jephthah opens with the standard phrase: 'Again the Israelites did evil in the eyes of the LORD' (Judg. 10:6). The list of idols that follows is testimony to the depths to which Israel had sunk. Instead of worshipping the true God, they turned to every false god available to them. Then, when the inevitable oppression came and they cried out to God, His response was to suggest they try calling on their idols to save them instead! So for eighteen years they were 'shattered and crushed' (10:8) by the Ammonites, until God's mercy finally won through and He raised up another judge: Jephthah.

Like Abimelech, Jephthah was an outcast, being of illegitimate parentage and not a full Israelite. Unlike Abimelech, however, he did not seek to be made king. Instead, it was the local elders who begged him to lead them. Eventually, after checking the small print, Jephthah agreed, and immediately entered into negotiations with the Ammonite king.

What a contrast this is to Abimelech! Where his predecessor had schemed and murdered to become king, and sought revenge at the slightest provocation, Jephthah, who suffered a similar background, had to be persuaded to lead the people, and instead of turning to violence he sought first to negotiate for peace.

The Ammonite king replied by explaining that all Israel needed to do was to give them back their land from across the Jordan. Jephthah's considered response – a whole thirteen verses long – was basically, 'I see where you've got confused. That land actually belonged to the Amorites, not the Ammonites. An easy mistake, but not one that matters since God *gave* us the land. If you really want it you'll be fighting against Him, so I suggest you reconsider!'

The Vow, the Victory and the Virgin

The result? War! And as Jephthah had promised, God was fighting on Israel's side, as we are told, 'the Spirit of the LORD came on Jephthah' (11:29).

And then came the vow ...

'If you give the Ammonites into my hands, whatever comes out of the door of my house to meet me when I return in triumph from the Ammonites will be the LORD's, and I will sacrifice it as a burnt offering' (11:30–31). Now unless it was customary for Jephthah to be greeted at home by a goat or bull or the like, this can really only be read as an offer of human sacrifice. So what is going on? One moment he is this godly follower of Yahweh, then the next he offers to make a human sacrifice, something which was expressly forbidden in Deuteronomy 18:10. So when Jephthah unsurprisingly crushed the Ammonites, and he came home to be greeted by his daughter, the big question is: did Jephthah kill her?

Those who believe he did look to the fact that he promised her as a burnt offering, and reacted with such horror at seeing his daughter emerge from the house. Not only that but, ironically, Chemosh, the god of the Ammonites, demanded human sacrifice.

Against Jephthah killing his daughter, however, is his relationship with God: and that a 'burnt offering' could simply imply his daughter being completely given over to God, maybe in lifelong service at the tabernacle. Note also the fact that she bewailed her virgin status rather than her impending death.

Regardless of whether or not he killed her, Jephthah's rash promise cost him his daughter and his lineage. But in stark contrast to the Israelites, he was at least faithful to his word!

Judges 9–21

Discussion Starters

1. What struck you most from the account of Jephthah's judgeship?

2. The Israelites worshipped every false god available in Canaan and the surrounding lands, yet still considered themselves to be God's chosen people. How can we avoid the trap of thinking we worship God, while we are really consumed by the things the world tells us are important?

3. Despite their wholesale idolatry, we are told God 'could bear Israel's misery no longer' (10:16). Read Psalm 145:8 and James 5:10–11. What do these things tell us about God, especially in His relationship with us?

4. The envy of the Ephraimites in chapter 12 led to 42,000 of them being slaughtered: by other Israelites! Read Proverbs 14:30, 1 Corinthians 13:4 and James 3:16. Why do you think envy is so strongly condemned in Scripture?

The Vow, the Victory and the Virgin

WEEK TWO

5. Although God was with Jephthah and he expressed great faith ('Let the Lord, the Judge, decide the dispute this day …', 11:27), he still decided to make his rash vow. Why do you think he did this?

6. Unlike the idol-loving Israelites, Jephthah was faithful to his word (whether or not that meant putting his daughter to death), but his promise to God was tragically flawed. What can we learn from his example? (Consider Ecclesiastes 5:2–5.)

7. By contrast, God's promises are perfect. What promises has He given to you, whether universal promises for the Church or individual promises for your life?

Judges 9-21

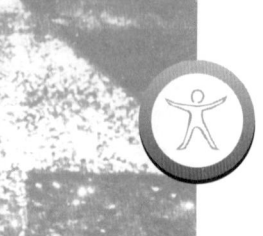

Personal Application

Everyone makes promises – sometimes with much prayerful consideration, and at other times entirely on the spur of the moment. The problem is that we cannot be certain of fulfilling our promises. Even something as simple as promising to buy a child an ice cream may, for reasons outside your control, be prevented. By contrast, when God promised Abraham that he would have a son even though that seemed impossible (see Gen. 17:15–17), Paul tells us that Abraham was 'fully persuaded that God had power to do what he had promised' (Rom. 4:21).

So even as we are faced with our own limitations, they should encourage us to look to God who is the only one able to fulfil His promises. The question is: do we really believe that God's promises are best?

Seeing Jesus in the Scriptures

God's promise to Abraham was more than just a son. In Genesis 22 He said, 'Through your offspring all nations on earth will be blessed' (Gen. 22:18). This singular 'offspring' was God's promised Messiah – Jesus, God's own Son. According to some scholars there are over 300 Old Testament prophecies that relate to Jesus. He is the greatest of all promises!

God's promise to Abraham was fulfilled when Jesus came to earth to save all who put their trust in Him. But it is not over yet … There are still many prophecies to be brought to pass, many promises yet to be fulfilled. One day Jesus will come again. We have already seen He is coming to bring justice, but He has promised so much more!

WEEK 3

Samson's Great Strength

Opening Icebreaker

Wink murder – a fitting game when looking at Judges! Take as many cards as there are people, with only one card being an ace, and place them face down. Whoever selects the ace is the 'murderer', and their job is to 'kill' as many people as possible by winking at them. When a person is winked at, they must fall down 'dead'. A live player can accuse the 'murderer', but if they are wrong they automatically 'die'. The game ends when the 'murderer' is discovered.

Bible Readings

- Judges 13:1–15:20 (or if short of time, 13:1–8; 15:1–20)
- Numbers 6:1–21
- 2 Timothy 3:16–17
- Proverbs 19:21
- James 4:13–15
- Romans 11:29

Key Verse: '… you will conceive and give birth to a son … a Nazirite, set apart to God from birth, and he will begin the deliverance of Israel from the hands of the Philistines.' (13:5)

Focus: There is nothing inherently wrong with making plans, but God's plans are best.

Judges 9-21

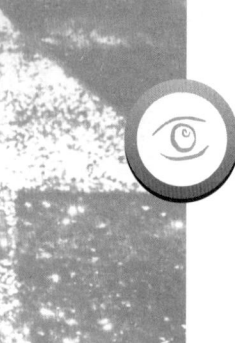

Opening Our Eyes

For the final time we read that 'the Israelites did evil in the eyes of the LORD' (Judg. 13:1), and for forty years God handed them over to the most famous of their oppressors: the Philistines. The standard cycle of Judges breaks down at this point though, as, instead of the expected crying out to the Lord, the Israelites remain silent. In chapter 15 it becomes apparent that they have simply accepted their situation as the men of Judah said, 'Don't you realise that the Philistines are rulers over us?' (v.11).

Despite this, God played out His part in the cycle anyway, and set in motion His plan of liberation, raising up the most famous of the judges: Samson. God promised a barren Danite woman: '… you will conceive and give birth to a son … the boy is to be a Nazirite, set apart to God from birth, and he will begin the deliverance of Israel from the hands of the Philistines' (13:5). Note that he would only 'begin' the deliverance, not complete it. Samson would be the first judge to fail to liberate Israel from oppression, and it would not be until the rise of Samuel that 'the Philistines were subdued and did not invade Israelite territory again' (1 Sam. 7:13).

Samson was to be brought up as a Nazirite (literally 'consecrated one'), and the fact that his parents did not know what this entailed hammers home the failure of the Israelites to pass on the teaching about God to the next generation. The rules for Nazirites are clearly laid out in Numbers 6:1–21:

- They were to consume no produce of the vine.
- They were to have no razor taken to their hair.
- They were to avoid all close contact with corpses.

As Samson's story unfolds, however, it becomes clear that he did not really care about being a Nazirite and, in the end, he broke *all* these rules.

Many of the stories in these chapters may be familiar to us: Samson's marriage to the Philistine woman, despite his parents' objections; his Spirit-empowered slaughter of a lion; his squabble with the Philistines, which ended with him killing thirty of them; his burning of the Philistine crops, which led to them killing his in-laws; his killing of more Philistines which ended in them threatening the tribe of Judah; and finally his slaughter of a further 1,000 Philistines using only a donkey's jawbone!

What may not be so familiar is that Samson's story goes through cycles in much the same way as Israel's. In fact, in many ways, Samson is a parallel of the nation of Israel. God brought both into being through miraculous births, He called both to be set apart for Him, He gave both a clear set of rules for life, He empowered both by His presence, He gave both a calling to bring salvation. And despite all this, both Samson and Israel failed God repeatedly, pursuing their own selfish desires, and getting caught in the downward spiral to destruction.

Just as Israel kept breaking her covenant with God, Samson broke his Nazirite vow by surrounding himself with corpses and drinking wine ('feast' in 14:10 specifically implies the consumption of wine). And even when Samson fulfilled his call to wipe out Philistines, he only killed them out of personal revenge, rather than any sense of being led by the Lord.

Amazingly, though, despite Samson's flagrant disregard for his Nazirite restrictions, the Spirit of the Lord *still* gave him incredible strength and God *still* used him to judge the Philistines!

Judges 9–21

Discussion Starters

1. What stood out most for you in this first half of the account of Samson's life?

2. Manoah and his wife did not know how to carry out God's instruction for their son, because they were not sure of the details of the Nazirite vow in the Law. What can we learn from this about the need for Christians today to know what the Bible says? (Consider 2 Timothy 3:16–17.)

3. 'The Spirit of the Lord came upon' Samson three times: to kill a lion (14:6), to kill thirty Philistines (14:19) and then to kill a further 1,000 Philistines (15:14). How does this line up with your understanding or experience of being empowered by the Spirit?

4. Samson constantly rebelled again his God-given status, and used his gift of strength entirely for his own ends. Why do you think God continued to give Samson power? (Consider Romans 11:29.)

Samson's Great Strength

5. Read Judges 14:4. Can you think of other instances, either in the Bible or in your experience, where people were used by God without them realising?

6. The events in these chapters could appear to be simply a series of coincidences. It takes faith to see God's hand at work, bringing His plans to fruition through people's actions, even when they cannot see it themselves. Can you think of ways in which God has similarly been working out His plans in your life and the lives of others?

7. Samson was given everything – a miraculous birth, set apart for God, a clear calling and superhuman strength – but he failed to actively use his calling, gifts or blessings for God. How can we ensure we do not fall into the same trap?

Judges 9–21

Personal Application

Making plans is natural – we all do it! Sometimes we make plans purely for our own benefit or for the benefit of others. At other times we make plans to bring honour and glory to God.

There is nothing inherently wrong with making plans. The problem comes when we start trusting in our plans and our ability to fulfil them instead of trusting God and submitting to *His* plans. James 4 warns us to avoid this trap: 'Why, you do not even know what will happen tomorrow … you ought to say, "If it is the Lord's will, we will live and do this or that"' (James 4:14–15).

Proverbs 19:21 says, 'Many are the plans in a man's heart, but it is the LORD's purpose that prevails.' His plans *always* come to pass. But can we really trust that God's plans are the best?

Seeing Jesus in the Scriptures

In the previous session, we considered the many prophecies about Jesus – God's promises to provide a Saviour for His people. This is God's amazing plan of salvation that can be seen on every page of Scripture. As with all God's plans, it was put into motion 'at just the right time' (Rom. 5:6). God Himself came to earth as a human, giving His life in return for ours.

In the words of the hymn 'See What a Morning': 'See God's salvation plan, wrought in love, borne in pain, paid in sacrifice, fulfilled in Christ, the Man, for He lives: Christ is risen from the dead!'

WEEK 4

Samson's Great Weakness

Opening Icebreaker

Can you think of things which we take for granted, yet can cause real problems when they fail? For example, I was once transporting a pig to the abattoir along a busy road when I noticed it was half hanging out of the side of the trailer, seemingly enjoying the view! It turned out that a single, small rivet that I had not even noticed before had broken off, and it could have caused a serious accident. Thankfully, it all worked out fine in the end … well, maybe not for the pig!

Bible Readings

- Judges 16 (if short of time just read Judges 16:4–21)
- Judges 15:18
- 2 Corinthians 12:9–10
- Judges 3:7–11
- Hebrews 11:32

Key Verse: 'He awoke from his sleep and thought, "I'll go out as before and shake myself free." But he did not know that the LORD had left him.' (16:20)

Focus: It is very natural for us to have desires, but God's desires are best.

25

Judges 9-21

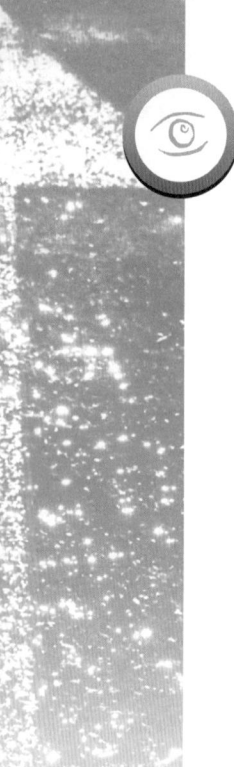 **Opening Our Eyes**

As we come into the last curve of Judges' downward spiral, we find Samson deep in Philistine territory. As usual, Samson was not there to satisfy God's desire to free Israel, but to satisfy his own desires in the local brothel! Seizing their chance to finally capture him, the Philistines surrounded the brothel and waited for Samson to emerge.

And emerge he did, ripping off the massive gates of the city and carrying them forty miles into Judah's territory – a task whose immensity was only surpassed by its utter pointlessness! Once again Samson had used his God-given strength entirely for his own ends.

The following story, of Samson and Delilah, is probably the most famous in the whole book, yet it is also undoubtedly the most tragic. Samson fell in love with this Philistine woman, who in turn fell in love with money. The amount offered her by the Philistines was equivalent to around twenty-five years of average earnings. All she had to do was find out the source of Samson's great strength.

It is interesting to note that they thought his strength was supernatural, so Samson could not have been some huge, muscle-bound strongman, as he is often depicted, otherwise the source of his strength would have been obvious!

Delilah's first few attempts to coax out his secret were met with magical-sounding red herrings: being tied with fresh bowstrings and bound with new ropes. He even got dangerously close to the truth, telling her to weave his hair into a cloth. Finally, though, when these failed to sap Samson's strength, the nagging began in earnest and 'she prodded him day after day until he was tired to death' (16:16). So Samson told her about his hair!

Samson's Great Weakness

WEEK FOUR

Verse 20 of Judges 16 is one of the most heartbreaking verses in the Bible, as the now bald Samson leapt up to fight the Philistines, saying, '"I'll go out as before and shake myself free." But he did not know that the LORD had left him.' His rejection of his calling and his final betrayal of the Nazirite vow had cut him off from God, the source of his strength. As the Philistines bound and blinded him, he was powerless to resist.

And so it looks like the end for Samson, the last of the judges in this book. How far we have come since the exemplary reign of Othniel who worked as one with the Lord to free Israel. Samson was a self-centred, unfaithful, ungodly judge, and ended up blinded, imprisoned and an object of ridicule ...

'But the hair on his head began to grow again after it had been shaved' (16:22). Suddenly we realise, God had not finished with him yet! Samson may have spent his time and his gifts in pursuit of his own desires, but now we see that God had also been pursuing His desires. And now He had His man exactly where He wanted him – standing by the supporting pillars of the great temple of the Philistine god, Dagon. Although Samson's prayer in verse 28 is entirely self-centred, as was his only other prayer in Judges 15:18, God again granted his request, and down came the temple, killing thousands of Philistines.

So the final cycle of Judges grinds to a halt with Israel still under the iron fist of the Philistines. The land will not know peace again until God raises up a king whose desires match His own!

Judges 9-21

 **Discussion Starters**

1. What struck you from this well-known account of Samson's downfall?

2. Samson is often presented as a 'type' of Christ (meaning he can be compared with Jesus in role, action and situation), and he is listed among the faithful in Hebrews 11:32. What in Samson's life could be considered faithful or could be compared to Jesus?

3. The Spirit of the Lord came on Samson four times – more than any other judge. Yet after losing his hair he was unaware that the Lord had left him. How can you tell when you are acting in your own strength as opposed to acting in the power of the Spirit?

4. Remind yourself of the brief account of Othniel in Judges 3:7–11. Othniel and the Lord worked together in perfect partnership with the same desires. How did Samson's desires and those of God differ or match?

Samson's Great Weakness

_____
_____

5. Samson's clashes with the Philistines were always self-centred, and yet the Lord used him to begin the judgment against this oppressor. Clearly God can use us, even if our desires are misplaced, but how can we tell if we have mixed motives when we are serving Him? And does it really matter if we have mixed motives?

_____
_____
_____
_____

6. Read Samson's two prayers in Judges 15:18 and 16:28, both of which were granted by God. What can we learn from these entirely self-centred prayers?

_____
_____
_____
_____

7. Samson's main area of weakness was his desire for women. While our own areas of weakness may be different from his, we still have them all the same. How can we guard ourselves against being ensnared by our sinful desires as Samson was?

_____
_____
_____
_____

Judges 9-21

Personal Application

We all have desires – some of them good and godly, others twisted and sinful. Like Samson our sinful desires can lead us astray if we allow them, and we can end up being enslaved by them. However, even in the most desperate of such situations, when we feel defeated and unable to win the battle against temptation, or even to fight, God can still use us. Paul said, 'For when I am weak, then I am strong' (2 Cor. 12:10), because at such times we are often of most use to God.

Samson is praised in Hebrews 11 for his faith, despite the fact it is barely perceptible in this account in Judges! And God still used him to fulfil *His* desires to begin the liberation of Israel. Imagine what God can do with us and a little faith that His desires really are the best!

Seeing Jesus in the Scriptures

Hebrews 4:15 tells us that Jesus was tempted just like us, but He never gave way to any sinful desires. Instead, Jesus' desire was to do God's will. Although Samson was quite different in this regard, he is often considered similar to Jesus in many ways. Both their births were prophesied by angels. Both were set apart for God from birth. Both suffered opposition, even from their own people. And both were captured and tortured, giving their lives to free God's people from oppression.

And just as Samson appeared to have failed as he was led away, bald and blind, Jesus seemed defeated as He hung on the cross, dying and deserted. But, what looked like failure was in fact the greatest work of liberation in history!

WEEK 5

The Trouble with Idols

Opening Icebreaker

'Would you rather?' is a very simple game where the group is given two options to choose between, and they vote on which they would rather. (For example: 'Would you rather never play, or always lose?') Either make up options, source them from the internet or use those in the leader's notes for this session on pages 57–58.

Bible Readings

- Judges 17:1–18:31
  (if short of time just read Judges 17:1–18:1; 18:16–26)
- Leviticus 10:8–11
- Romans 7:6
- Judges 2:10–11
- Galatians 1:10

Key Verse: 'Micah said, "Now I know that the LORD will be good to me, since this Levite has become my priest."' (17:13)

Focus: While everyone may be entitled to their own opinion, God's opinion is best.

Opening Our Eyes

Having completed the six cycles of the major judges, the book closes with two accounts from this period that demonstrate the depths to which Israel had sunk. These stories do not follow on from the time of Samson, but actually take place around the time of Othniel and Ehud. As such it is a startling reminder of the statement in Judges 2:10: 'After that whole generation had been gathered to their fathers, another generation grew up, who knew neither the LORD nor what he had done for Israel.'

This first story opens with a man called Micah, who had robbed a massive sum of money from his own mother. Scared of being cursed by her, Micah returned her silver, but it is not his outrageous behaviour that surprises us; rather it is his mother's response to receiving back her stolen goods. 'I solemnly consecrate my silver to the LORD for my son to make a carved image and a cast idol' (Judg. 17:3). In the same breath, she uses the covenant name of God, yet completely disregards the second commandment: 'You shall not make for yourself an idol in the form of anything in heaven above or on the earth beneath or in the waters below. You shall not bow down to them or worship them' (Exod. 20:4–5). Seemingly unaware of this irony, Micah did as she suggested and set up his own pagan temple, dedicated to the Lord. Amazingly they thought this was the right thing to do!

Some time later, a Levite turned up, whom the narrator will later reveal was none other than Moses' grandson (see Judg. 18:30), and so Micah seizes the opportunity to hire him. What a result! Now he had a real, proper Levite for his pagan temple. Again, Micah thought this was the right thing to do: 'Now I know the LORD will be good to me, since this Levite has become my priest' (17:13). The events that followed, however, suggest otherwise!

The Trouble with Idols

Chapter 18 opens with the Danites looking for a place to live. Back in Judges 1, they came bottom of the league when the tribes were trying to take the land: 'The Amorites confined the Danites to the hill country, not allowing them to come down into the plain' (v.34).

Like Moses and Joshua in the preceding generations, the Danites sent spies to check out the land, and in the process they sought guidance from the Lord at Micah's pagan temple. The Levite's response was positive and, whether or not this was from God, his words were soon proved correct as the spies came across the idyllic region of Laish: '... they saw that the people were living in safety, like the Sidonians, unsuspecting and secure. And since their land lacked nothing, they were prosperous' (Judg. 18:7).

When the spies reported back, the Danites immediately sent out an army of 600 men to seize Laish. On their way, they stopped off again at Micah's house, this time to steal his idols and his priest, which the Levite was quite pleased about. Micah was not so pleased, but when he went to confront the Danites, they basically told him to stop complaining or they would kill him.

So in the end Micah lost all his religious paraphernalia that he thought was so valuable. Meanwhile, the thieving Danites wiped out the peace-loving people of Laish and settled down with their new idol cult, clearly of the opinion that they also were doing what was right!

Judges 9–21

Discussion Starters

1. What struck you most in this tale of Micah and his idols?

2. The opinion of the characters in this story was clearly that they were doing what God wanted – things that were 'right'. Which of their actions, however, are contrary to God's opinion as revealed in Scripture?

3. By doing what seemed right, Micah believed he would secure God's blessing. Even the grandson of Israel's lawgiver, Moses, joined in this farce – all of them using God's covenant name while breaking His covenant laws! How could they be so badly mistaken?

4. Read Leviticus 10:8–11. It is no coincidence that the two stories in the epilogue to Judges revolve around the actions of Levites, because they were the ones responsible for teaching the Law to the people, a duty in which they had clearly failed. Whom do you consider is responsible today for ensuring that we are aware of what the Bible teaches?

The Trouble with Idols

5. Romans 7:6 talks about the 'new way of the Spirit' in contrast to 'the old way of the written code'. What do you think this means for Christians today as we seek to do what is right?

6. Can you think of occasions when Christians have incorrectly assumed they are living God's way? How can we guard ourselves against such mistaken opinions?

7. We do not only have to battle with our own opinions, but often we want to live up to the opinions and expectations of others as well. Share examples from your own experience where people's actions have been shaped by the opinions of others, rather than God's opinion.

Judges 9–21

Personal Application

It can be so easy to fall into the trap of trying to do things that look good to others and to ourselves. This is not always wrong, but concern about the opinions of others can be detrimental to our walk with God – indeed we may even convince ourselves that we are serving God when in fact we are simply looking to please others. In Galatians 1:10, Paul wrote, 'Am I now trying to win the approval of human beings, or of God? Or am I trying to please people? If I were still trying to please people, I would not be a servant of Christ.' We have not been called to do what looks 'right' to us or to anyone else; we have been called to do what God says is right. But can we really have faith that God's opinion is always best?

Seeing Jesus in the Scriptures

In Week 4 we saw that Jesus' one desire was to do God's will – to fulfil His plan and promise for His people. But on the evening before His execution, we see Jesus in conflict as He prayed in the Garden of Gethsemane. So much so that He sweated drops of blood! Yet, as He knelt before God, He said these amazing words: 'Father, if you are willing, take this cup from me; yet not my will, but yours be done' (Luke 22:42). What a statement of absolute faith in God's will. And, having submitted Himself to God so gloriously, He went to meet His betrayer.

WEEK 6

The Best Will in the World

Opening Icebreaker

In Numbers 22, God spoke to Balaam using a donkey! How many other ways can you think of that God speaks to people, whether in the Bible or in your own experience?

Bible Readings

- Judges 19:1–20:48
  (if short of time just read Judges 20:1–25, 46–48)
- Psalm 23
- John 10:3–4
- John 16:13
- Romans 8:28

Key Verse: 'The Israelites went up to Bethel and enquired of God. They said, "Who of us shall go first to fight against the Benjamites?" The LORD replied, "Judah shall go first."' (20:18)

Focus: We have been given free will, but God's will is best and we need to discern what His will is for our lives.

Judges 9-21

Opening Our Eyes

This second epilogue opens with a Levite and his concubine (a wife with no marital rights) spending the night in the Benjamite city of Gibeah. During the night 'some of the wicked men of the city' (19:22) surrounded their house and demanded that the Levite be brought out so they could 'know' him. The Levite, disgracing himself as a priest and husband, threw his concubine out into the street, leaving the men to take out their frustrations on her instead.

In the morning he found her lifeless body on the doorstep. Not to be outdone by the horror of the Benjamites, the Levite then cut up the corpse and mailed it off to the other tribes of Israel with a demand for justice.

The Israelites were outraged and chapter 20 opens with them raising an army. 'Then, when the army arrives at Gibeah in Benjamin, it can give them what they deserve for all this vileness done in Israel' (20:10). They next demanded that the tribe of Benjamin hand over the men of Gibeah. In response, however, the Benjamites instead gathered to defend their kinsmen, and suddenly the whole nation was plunged into civil war. Clearly, it was time to find out what God wanted them to do!

'The Israelites went up to Bethel and enquired of God. They said, "Who of us shall go first to fight against the Benjamites?" The LORD replied, "Judah shall go first"' (20:18). Somehow this feels like the wrong question. Surely there is a step missing here somewhere. They came to God, not asking whether they should go to battle, but who should go to battle first – they had already made up their minds to fight! God responded much as He had in the opening verses of Judges by sending Judah. This time, however, their enemy was not the Canaanites, but their own brother tribe of Benjamin.

The Best Will in the World

Looking at the line-up, you can imagine that perhaps the Israelites did not feel the need to ask whether to fight or not, as their army was almost fifteen times larger than that of Benjamin. Their victory was a foregone conclusion, surely – no need to seek God about such a trifling matter. And yet the coalition force took a colossal beating, losing 22,000 men in one day.

Clearly the Israelites learned from their mistake, as this time they asked God whether they should actually fight. He answered, 'Go up against them' (20:23).

While God's approval of this civil war may come as something of a surprise, that is as nothing compared to the surprise of the Israelites as they went up against the soldiers of Benjamin the next day and received another thrashing with 18,000 men killed!

Now this is an interesting development. The Israelites seemed to have everything on their side now that they had sought God's will, and yet they were defeated a second time. Was this truly God's will? Would God really call His people to fight among themselves with thousands slain?

With much weeping and wailing, the Israelites sought the Lord again and this time He promised to give the soldiers of Benjamin into their hands. And so Gibeah fell. Not only Gibeah, but *all* the cities of Benjamin, until finally all that remained of that once great tribe was 600 men.

And so one of the twelve tribes of Israel was brought to the brink of extinction – and all because one Levite sacrificed his concubine to save his own skin!

Judges 9-21

Discussion Starters

1. What struck you most in this story of the ungodly behaviour of the Israelites?

2. When you consider what God's people have been up to in these two chapters, one might expect God to have turned His face away. Yet the moment they called on Him, He responded. What does this tell you about God? Does this match up to your own experience?

3. When they finally sought God's will, He told the Israelites to go into battle even though it would result in defeat with thousands being killed. How might the outcome of this story affect how you trust God?

4. Do you think God ever calls us to go through things which are painful and even result in tragedy and failure?

5. God had given the Israelites the Law, which told them how to deal with the men of Gibeah, but when the situation changed, they failed to ask God what they should do. Can you think of situations when you have needed to seek God's will beyond what He has revealed in the Bible?

6. How have you personally received God's guidance?

7. When the Israelites finally enquired of the Lord, His reply was clear. The words used of the Holy Spirit in John 16:13 show that speaking to us is one of His key roles. What advice would you give to Christians who struggle to discern or recognise God's voice?

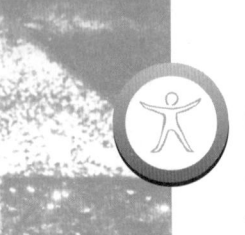

Personal Application

Not everything is as it appears! Only God sees how all things work together (Rom. 8:28), and although we may not like the idea, He may sometimes call us to things that either do not work or end with disaster. Tragedy, suffering and failure, however, are as important a part of following Jesus as are joy, triumph and success.

The important thing is to seek God's will and act accordingly, leaving everything else in His hands. Even the smallest of decisions are worth bringing to Him because this reminds us that there is no area of our lives He does not care about. We may never know the true significance of our actions, but can we still trust that God's will is best?

Seeing Jesus in the Scriptures

In John 10, Jesus refers to Himself as a shepherd with His followers being the sheep: '... the sheep listen to his voice. He calls his own sheep by name and leads them out ... He goes on ahead of them, and his sheep follow him because they know his voice' (vv.3–4). Similarly, in Psalm 23, David talks of the Lord as *his* shepherd.

Sheep rely on their shepherd for everything from food and water to protection and guidance. The same is true of us as Jesus' followers. How wonderful it is to know that we have the Lord as our shepherd, and though sometimes He leads us through dark valleys, it will always be for His glory and our good. His will really is the best will in the world!

WEEK 7

Marriage Vows

Opening Icebreaker

We have seen a number of strange events on our journey through Judges, but the oddest in the Bible has to be 2 Kings 2:23–25. Here, the prophet Elisha is mocked by a group of boys for being bald. His response? He cursed the boys, and a couple of bears came and mauled forty-two of the youths! Can you think of other stories in the Bible that are bizarre or funny?

Bible Readings

- Judges 21
- Judges 1:6
- Deuteronomy 7:2
- Isaiah 55:8–9
- Revelation 7:14

Key Verse: 'In those days Israel had no king; everyone did as he saw fit.' (21:25)

Focus: Our ways may seem good to us, but God's ways are best.

Judges 9-21

Opening Our Eyes

In the previous session we left the tribe of Benjamin reduced to 600 men without a single woman to carry on the tribal line! Usually that would not present a problem as there were plenty of other Israelite women available. Unfortunately the other tribes had made a vow that 'Not one of us will give his daughter in marriage to a Benjamite' (Judg. 21:1).

The vow itself is somewhat understandable, considering the anger the other Israelites must have felt towards this tribe who had defended the rape and murder of a Levite's concubine. No doubt we have all had knee-jerk reactions when outraged. It probably seemed right at the time, and yet in hindsight the Israelites were distraught at being reduced to eleven tribes.

Thankfully, another rash vow came to their aid, 'that anyone who failed to assemble before the LORD at Mizpah should certainly be put to death' (21:5). And so they hatched their cunning plan! The people of Jabesh-Gilead had not turned up to punish the Benjamites, so the Israelites punished them in return sparing only 400 virgins whom they gave as wives for the Benjamites.

They solved the problem of the other 200 men with another loophole. Instead of *giving* their daughters in marriage, the men of Shiloh were forced to allow their daughters to be stolen by the remaining Benjamite bachelors!

The two bookends to these closing epilogues of Judges are 'In those days ... everyone did as he saw fit' (Judg. 17:6; 21:25) or more literally 'in his own eyes each man did the right thing'. The Israelites had taken these oaths because they seemed right at the time. Then they

Marriage Vows

had used loopholes in those oaths to ensure the tribe of Benjamin did not die out. How can that not be right? And yet, the result was the death of thousands of Israelites, the destruction of a whole community of men, women and children, and the rape of hundreds of women – hardly a fitting outcome!

And these things took place within a generation of the death of Joshua. How quickly Israel forgot the Lord and His ways! Back in the opening chapter of Judges, as the tribes of Judah and Simeon began to drive out the Canaanites, we read in verse 6 of their mercy toward Adoni-Bezek, merely cutting off his thumbs and big toes rather than putting him to death. And yet God had told them to show the Canaanites no mercy. This is where it all began, failing to follow God's ways, and so the downward spiral.

Where is God in all this? He is hardly mentioned in this chapter, and mostly only when people are complaining to Him. Although it is hard to see how the tribe of Benjamin would have been saved without the bloodthirsty solutions of the other tribes, God still had plans for them. Through Benjamin, God would give Israel her first king. When the kingdom split into Israel and Judah after the reign of Solomon, Benjamin would join Judah and so escape the scattering of the ten northern tribes. And through Benjamin God would raise up Paul, the great apostle to the Gentiles.

So, despite the fact that the Israelites committed such atrocities, in the belief their ways were the right ways, we see that behind all this God's ways prevail, and if there is one thing the book of Judges has taught us, it is surely that we can have faith that God's ways *really* are the best!

Judges 9-21

Discussion Starters

1. What did you find most striking in this final chapter of Judges?

_____
_____
_____
_____

2. The Israelites were so enraged by the tribe of Benjamin that they made vows which they later regretted. Can you think of occasions when you have felt anger or indignation that could have resulted in similarly rash vows?

_____
_____
_____
_____

3. When Dan set up a cult worshipping Micah's idols in chapter 18, none of the Israelites opposed them. Yet when a woman was raped and murdered the whole nation rose up to punish those involved. Share examples in the Church today where our reaction might be disproportionate to God's.

_____
_____
_____
_____

4. Three times in these two epilogues the narrator points out that there was no king over the Israelites at this time. In the books of Kings (which may have had the same author as Judges) the whole nation is judged according to how the kings rule them – whether or not they do what is right in God's eyes. What then might, or might not, be the advantages of having a king?

5. Read Deuteronomy 7:2 and compare this command with the actions of Judah in Judges 1:6. We would probably consider showing mercy to always be the right thing to do, but in this instance it was not. In light of this, how can we be sure what God's ways are?

6. Read Isaiah 55:8–9. How can we grow in our faith that God's ways really are best, when at times they are so much higher than ours, and even sometimes seem contrary to what is right in our own eyes or in the eyes of others?

7. What do you feel are the most important things that the book of Judges has to teach Christians today?

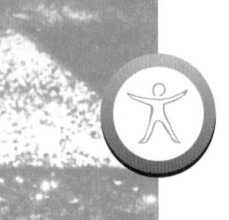

Personal Application

As we have journeyed through these closing chapters of Judges, we have seen again and again that God's ways are best. His justice is best, because He sees all outcomes. His promises are best, because He has the power to fulfil them. His plans are best, because they work for His glory and our good. His desires are best, because He alone is good. His opinion is best, because He cannot be swayed by the expectation of others. His will is best, because what is right in His eyes is pure and perfect!

However, our journey is far from over. We will only grow in our faith that God's ways are best as we actively trust and submit to Him, and start to walk in His ways. Only then will we experience the wonder of learning to live God's way.

Seeing Jesus in the Scriptures

Although we leave the people of Israel still awaiting their king, we can rejoice that we already have our king – the best king, our perfect king, Jesus! Perfect in justice, perfect in faith, perfect in submission, perfect in every way.

Speaking about Jesus, John wrote these words in Revelation 17:14: 'They will make war against the Lamb, but the Lamb will overcome them because he is Lord of lords and King of kings – and with him will be his called, chosen and faithful followers.' This is the promise we hope in, the fulfilment of God's great plan, that one day we will live with Him forever, and together we will cry, 'Jesus is King!'

Leader's Notes

These notes are designed to help lead these sessions in a group. Please do read through the notes before each session to help with your preparation. It is also worth reading through the Personal Application and Seeing Jesus in the Scriptures sections to get a feel for the direction of the session in question.

The overarching theme is that God's ways are best, and each session contrasts our ways with His.

Week 1: Abimelech: The Man who would be King

This session brings us to the first contrast between us and God. The issue here is justice. Our thirst for justice could better be thought of as seeking revenge, while God's justice is pure, perfect and will ultimately come to pass.

Opening Icebreaker

The aim of this icebreaker is to show that it is natural to want justice. It is worth finding a few more examples, such as the international fast food chain which was sued for the coffee being hot!

Bible Readings

All the sessions in this book have a number of verses from other parts of the Bible. It is not necessary to read these together at the beginning, as they are mainly used in the Discussion Starters, but it would be beneficial to read the main passage together. As this session covers one of the longer chapters in Judges, it may be best to read through the key sections shown in brackets, and ask the group to read the whole passage before you meet together.

Key Verse

This verse gives us the behind-the-scenes view, showing us that the ultimate source of the downfall of Abimelech and Shechem was God's justice.

Discussion Starters

1. This open question, encouraging people to share what was most striking for them from the passage, will be the starter for all sessions. The aim here is to encourage people to start talking, so it is worth trying to avoid getting bogged down with details or going into much depth.

3. In defining these two terms, we could describe justice as being based on what is morally right and fair, while revenge has more to do with paying back for an injury or wrong (whether real or imagined). Some of the icebreaker examples may be helpful as illustrations. It is worth discussing whether there is much overlap between the two, in which case a look at Exodus 21:22–25 may be of interest.

4. It is worth asking yourself this question beforehand so you can start the ball rolling with a considered response. Opinions will differ, but most people desire revenge at some level.

5. These verses are about God's ability to ensure justice is done regardless of human schemes and how situations appear.

6. This is not an easy question to tackle. It may help the discussion to talk about personal experiences of seeing God's justice at work either in the lives of those in the group or of others.

Leader's Notes

7. This type of question is often used as an attack on Christianity. The 'Personal Application' and 'Seeing Jesus in the Scriptures' sections go some way towards tackling it, but before the group read these, it is worth thrashing out this question for a while, especially if people have been faced with it themselves.

Week 2: The Vow, the Victory and the Virgin

This session compares human promises with God's promises, particularly focusing on the fact that not only are our promises often flawed, but also we cannot guarantee they will always be fulfilled. The subtle self-deceit of idol worship is also considered.

Opening Icebreaker

This only needs a little preparation beforehand to find a suitable object to throw to each other. Something soft that is easy both to throw and to catch would be best. The point of the icebreaker is that it is possible to think one thing, but actually do something completely different. This is specifically relevant for Discussion Starter 2.

Bible Readings

Since this session covers almost three chapters, the short sections in brackets only look at a small part of Jephthah's story. As his account is not that well known, it is important to encourage the group to read these three chapters *before* the session.

Key Verse

This is the point where Jephthah suddenly realises how foolish it was to make his rash promise to God.

Discussion Starters

1. As the vow and its outcome are such a major part of Jephthah's story, it is worth making sure the group does not spend too much time debating this, especially whether or not he killed his daughter.

2. The icebreaker may help illustrate the idea that it is possible to think one thing, yet do the opposite. How to avoid doing this in our walk with God could potentially give rise to a fairly lengthy discussion. Examining ourselves is important, and the issue of mixed motives will be considered in more depth in Week 5.

3. Following on from the previous Discussion Starter, these verses speak of the long-suffering nature of God's love and mercy. (It is interesting to note that James 5 goes on in verse 12 to consider making vows!)

4. It may be worth pointing out the difference between envy (coveting something that belongs to someone else) and jealousy (not wanting others to have what belongs to you). When detailing the Ten Commandments in Exodus 20, verse 5 describes God as jealous, while verse 17 prohibits coveting.

5. Opinions may be split over whether it was Jephthah's over-excitement or uncertainty that motivated him to make his vow. Another possible reason is that Jephthah was looking to ensure God's blessing by making his vow. Compare this with Jacob's manipulative promise in Genesis 28:20–22.

6. This is something of a two-sided question. On the one hand, Jephthah's faithfulness in keeping his vow (Num. 30:2) is an example for us, yet on the other, the horrific result of his rash promise serves as a sober warning for us. Ecclesiastes 5:2–5 talks about not being too hasty in what

Leader's Notes

we say. In the final session we will look more at the problems associated with making hasty promises, but the aim of this Discussion Starter is to see that our promises are imperfect.

7. It may be worth looking up a number of key promises in Scripture beforehand to get the ball rolling (eg John 3:16; Rom. 8:28; 1 John 1:9; Rev. 22:12). As people share personal promises they have received from God, this may provide a good opportunity to pray for one another.

Week 3: Samson's Great Strength

This session compares our plans with God's. Though there is nothing wrong with making plans, not only are we unable to guarantee them being carried out, but also we cannot always be certain they are in line with God's plans. However, even as we put our plans into action, we can be sure that God is at work bringing His perfect plans to pass. Knowledge of the Bible and the power of the Holy Spirit are also considered.

Opening Icebreaker

The point of this icebreaker is that there is one person behind what is going on, but it can be hard to work out who that person is. In a similar way, as we read the events of Samson's life we need to look carefully to realise God is actually the Person behind what is going on.

Key Verse

This verse sets the scene for Samson's narrative – not only that he must not cut his hair, but also that he would only 'begin' the work of judging the Philistines. God's plan for Samson's life was set before he was even born!

Discussion Starters

2. Although this question is not specifically introspective, it is worth encouraging people to question their own knowledge of and commitment to the Bible, and consider ways they can grow in this area. This may help to moderate the possible desire to bewail the general state of biblical knowledge in the Church today!

3. The focus here is on power, and while many people may want to shy away from the idea of the Holy Spirit empowering such violence, hopefully the expectation of receiving power from Him for all kinds of areas of life will come through. Verses like Romans 15:13 and Ephesians 3:16–17 may help as they speak of the inner working of power, not just the outward, visible signs.

If there is time, it may be a good opportunity to share personal experiences of the Holy Spirit's power at work.

4. Romans 11:29 states that 'God's gifts and his call are irrevocable'. This may help in the discussion, but this does not entirely answer the question. It is worth considering what God was doing through Samson despite the fact he used his strength so selfishly.

5. The most obvious biblical characters are those who do not know God. For example, in Exodus, Pharaoh was used by God to demonstrate His superiority to the Egyptian gods; and in the Gospels, Pontius Pilate was used to authorise Jesus' execution.

6. This is where the icebreaker links in – taking the time to actively look out for God's hand at work behind the scenes. It is worth having an example from your own experience that you can share to get the ball rolling. Some people may need more time to consider how God has worked in their lives, and it may help to encourage

Leader's Notes

people to share how they have seen God working through others in the group.

7. Rather than enter into a discussion about what people think of as their own calling or gifts or blessings, the focus here is really on how to avoid using any such things to glorify ourselves instead of God. In the next session we will look in more depth at examining our motives for the things we do.

Week 4: Samson's Great Weakness

Having looked at promises and plans, this session focuses on the desires that lie behind such things. In contrast to the pure desires of God, there is always a degree of mixed motives in our desires.

Opening Icebreaker

The point of this icebreaker is that there are probably many things we take for granted, from sitting in a chair or turning on a tap to driving through a green traffic light or over a level crossing. In the same way, Samson took his strength for granted ... until it was gone.

Key Verse

This is one of the most tragic verses in the Bible, as Samson assumed his strength would save him, but God had taken it away!

Discussion Starters

2. This should hopefully provoke some lively discussion, since at first glance Samson comes across as such a reprehensible individual that placing his actions alongside Jesus may seem absurd. However, in role Samson was

confident of his God-given strength, in action he was used by God in the salvation of His people, and in status he was set apart from birth and called by God. This Discussion Starter is not restricted to chapter 16, but takes into account the whole of the Samson narrative.

3. This is where the icebreaker links in, as it is quite possible to take the Holy Spirit's work for granted. There is the potential here for a fairly deep discussion, especially as you consider how you know when you are acting in the power of the Holy Spirit.

4. In Judges 3:9, the phrase 'who saved them' is a single Hebrew word: 'yoshiem' (literally 'he saved them'). The construction of this sentence is such that the saviour in question is deliberately ambiguous – it could be either Othniel or the Lord. In this way the narrator emphasises their perfect partnership in saving Israel. By contrast Samson's desires seem to have been the complete antithesis of God's.

5. There are two questions in this Discussion Starter, both focused on our motives. As discussing these may involve a certain amount of self-searching, it may be worth sharing an example from your own life of how God has used you despite your desires not being entirely in line with His. Failing this, a 'safe' example would be considering the motives of general groups of people. For example, many preachers admit they struggle with the desire for the acknowledgement and praise of their listeners, and yet they find God still uses them to change people's lives for His glory. Opinions may well differ on the value of actions with mixed motives, but even a little self-examination would reveal that completely pure motives are very rare!

6. Building on the previous Discussion Starter, mixed motives (or even entirely wrong motives!) in our prayers

Leader's Notes

may not necessarily mean God refuses to grant our requests. It may be worth considering some of the New Testament verses that talk about God granting prayers (eg Matt. 7:7–8; 21:22; Mark 11:24; and John 14:14).

7. Some people will not want to talk about their own area(s) of weakness, or would have a natural tendency to share those they consider 'safe' as opposed to what we might consider more serious sinful desires. However, the aim here is not necessarily to share specific weaknesses, but more to see that we all have them and so discuss how to guard ourselves against them. The focus should be more on solutions than on the problems.

This may also provide a good opportunity to pray for each other's struggles.

Week 5: The Trouble with Idols

This session focuses on the contrast between our and other people's opinions, and those of God.

Opening Icebreaker

The point of this icebreaker is to demonstrate that we do not all share the same opinions about everything, but neither do differing opinions have to mean only one is valid.

Here are ten 'Would you rather?' questions you could use for this icebreaker:
- Would you rather be poor and work at a job you love, or be rich and work at a job you hate?
- Would you rather never be able to clean your teeth, or never be able to clean your body?
- Would you rather be three foot taller or three foot shorter?

- Would you rather know everything or own everything?
- Would you rather be really hairy or completely bald?
- Would you rather have no internet or no car?
- Would you rather eat healthily or exercise regularly?
- Would you rather be super strong or super fast?
- Would you rather be stranded on an island alone or with someone you find really annoying?
- Would you rather be able to fly or be invisible?

Key Verse

This is another tragic verse, as Micah's opinion that God will bless him because he has a Levite to officiate at his pagan shrine is so ludicrously misguided.

Discussion Starters

2. The stealing, and the making and worshipping of idols are clearly contrary to God's will as revealed in the Ten Commandments (Exod. 20), but the slaughter of the Canaanite people of Laish and the seizing of their land is in line with God's command in Deuteronomy 7:2 to show them no mercy. The narrator, however, cleverly portrays the people of Laish as being the only 'good guys' in this story.

3. The next few Discussion Starters are related to Scripture. The heart of Micah's problem (and of the others in this story) was that he did not actually know what God's opinion was and his actions reflect this. Had he and the other Israelites been aware of the Law, they would have known what God required of them, rather than simply relying on their own opinion.

4. No doubt many people will place this responsibility first at the feet of church leaders, Christian authors and other Bible teachers. However, the aim of this Discussion Starter is to get to the point where people accept their own responsibility for their knowledge of the Bible.

Leader's Notes

It may be worth reminding the group of the discussion on biblical knowledge from Week 3.

5. This Discussion Starter may appear to be at odds with the previous three, which focus on Scripture as the source for what God says is best. However, Romans 7:6 actually builds on this. Scripture gives us an insight into God's opinion in many general areas of life, but often when it comes to specific situations this may not be sufficient, as often we are faced with choices that are all biblically acceptable. At such times we either rely on our own opinions or we rely on the guidance of the Holy Spirit.

This issue is also considered in Week 6, so it may be worth having a look at Discussion Starters 5 to 7 of Week 6 to avoid too much overlap.

6. Returning to the idea that it is possible to think you are doing what is right in God's eyes, when in fact it is only right in your own eyes, the second of the questions is the more important. This should also build on what the group has been discussing about guidance from Scripture and the Holy Spirit.

7. Encourage people to consider both sides of the issue, both doing things and *refraining from doing things* to live up to human opinions and expectations. For some this may be a significant problem and so may be painful to talk about. If so, this may be a good opportunity to spend some time praying for one another.

The Personal Application section also focuses on this issue.

Week 6: The Best Will in the World

WARNING: this is probably the most harrowing story in the whole of the book of Judges. A woman is raped until she dies and is then hacked up and her body parts sent around Israel! Behind this, however, we see a clear contrast between human will and God's will. The main focus of this session, then, is how to hear, recognise and discern what God's will is for our lives.

Opening Icebreaker

The aim of this icebreaker is to get people to think about the many ways in which God might choose to speak to people. Some examples in the Bible include: angels (Exod. 3:2), dreams (Gen. 20:3), visions (Acts 10:9–15), the ephod (1 Sam. 23:9–12) and an audible voice (1 Kings 19:12).

Key Verse

Having got into something of a mess, this is the point where the Israelites finally ask God what they should do - with shocking results!

Discussion Starters

1. Naturally the horrific fate of the Levite's concubine will have been the most notable thing. However, this is really only a small part of the events in these chapters, so it is worth encouraging the group to think about other things that caught their attention.

3. There may be some who really struggle with the idea that God would deliberately command His people to do something which resulted in such horrific defeat! It may be worth looking at some of the stories in the Bible where God's commands and actions seem to conflict with

Leader's Notes

our idea of how God works. For example, the devastation of Job or the deadly judgment of Ananias and Sapphira. The aim is to get to the point where the group can see that God doesn't always do what we expect.

4. Following on from the previous Discussion Starter, the focus here is on Christians today. Encouraging the group to share examples from their own lives may be of benefit in seeing how God has worked in each person's life, even during times of tragedy and failure.

5. In Discussion Starter 5 of the previous session, we looked at the 'new way of the Spirit', in Romans 7:6, contrasted with the 'old way of the written code'. It may be worth reminding the group of some of the points raised in that session to help as they consider personal examples of seeking God's will.

6. Continuing with the topic of being guided by God, this Discussion Starter offers more opportunities to share personal experiences.

In the icebreaker you spent some time thinking of different ways that God speaks and has spoken to people. In doing so, some may well have already mentioned ways they have received God's guidance. If not, it may be worth you starting things by sharing one of your own experiences of hearing from God.

7. John 16:13 says the Holy Spirit will 'guide ... speak ... and tell' – all of which imply verbal communication. There may be some in the group who struggle in this area, in which case this discussion is very important. One key point is that, since the Holy Spirit mostly speaks directly into our minds, He can easily be mistaken for our own thoughts. We do not necessarily recognise His voice by its sound, but rather by its content.

The question then becomes, 'How do we weigh this content?' Some guidelines include comparing with Scripture, looking for conviction and checking with wise, godly counsel. After we have done this, if we believe that we have discerned God's voice, it is also important to act upon what He has said in order to hopefully see if He really has spoken. In this way, we can better learn to recognise His voice.

Week 7: Marriage Vows

In this final session the book draws to a close with what at first glance may appear like a happy ending. However, the thin veneer of morality and godliness barely conceals the rotten core of life in Israel at this time. There is no happy ending, only a distressing sense of Israel's failure to learn to live God's way. The focus of this session is on the comparison between ways that seem right to us, and those which seem right to God, and how surprisingly far apart the two may be!

Opening Icebreaker

In the previous session the group considered the fact that God does not always speak and act as we might expect. The point of this icebreaker is to build on this by sharing some of the stranger and more outrageous stories from Scripture.

Key Verse

The second half of this verse is really the key phrase of the book of Judges. The Hebrew more literally says, 'in his own eyes each man did the right thing', and this emphasises the individualistic nature of the Israelites' actions.

Leader's Notes

Discussion Starters

2. This is a potentially more difficult Discussion Starter than most as what the group is being asked to share may not reflect well on them. If there is a reluctance to share, it may be worth broadening this out to thinking of other examples outside our own experience.

3. The point here is that, while the rape and murder of the concubine was certainly a wicked act that demanded justice, if anything the establishment of an idolatrous cult by an entire tribe was surely just as bad, if not worse, in God's eyes, since many people would have been ensnared by idol worship as a result. Similarly in the Church there can be a tendency to react strongly to things which seem particularly evil, while issues that could be considered more serious – such as the preaching of false doctrine – may end up being tolerated or even nurtured!

4. The need for godly leadership, and the problems associated with its lack, are the focus here. You may or may not decide to discuss this in some depth, but this would also be a good opportunity to pray for the leaders in your local church and even those in government.

5. In Deuteronomy 7:2, God gives the command that the Canaanites are to be wiped out and shown no mercy. There may well be some who, as in the previous session (specifically Discussion Starter 3), will struggle with the idea that God would give a command that appears contrary to His nature.

7. As the group's study of the book of Judges may have been spread over a fairly long period of time, it may be beneficial to remind the group of some of the topics that they have tackled since they began.

In book one the focus was on faith: what faith is and why it is so important; how faith is demonstrated through the way we live, and what can be achieved when, in faith, we work together with God; what things can damage our faith in God, and draw us away from keeping Him at the centre of our lives.

In book two the focus has been on God's ways: His justice, His promises, His plans, His desires, His opinions and His will. In addition to this we have considered the importance of knowing the Bible and recognising the Holy Spirit's guidance as we seek to live God's way in all situations.

National Distributors

UK: (and countries not listed below)

CWR, Waverley Abbey House, Waverley Lane, Farnham, Surrey GU9 8EP.
Tel: (01252) 784700 Outside UK (44) 1252 784700 Email: mail@cwr.org.uk

AUSTRALIA: KI Entertainment, Unit 21 317-321 Woodpark Road, Smithfield, New South Wales 2164.
Tel: 1 800 850 777 Fax: 02 9604 3699 Email: sales@kientertainment.com.au

CANADA: David C Cook Distribution Canada, PO Box 98, 55 Woodslee Avenue, Paris, Ontario N3L 3E5.
Tel: 1800 263 2664 Email: sandi.swanson@davidccook.ca

GHANA: Challenge Enterprises of Ghana, PO Box 5723, Accra.
Tel: (021) 222437/223249 Fax: (021) 226227 Email: ceg@africaonline.com.gh

HONG KONG: Cross Communications Ltd, 1/F, 562A Nathan Road, Kowloon.
Tel: 2780 1188 Fax: 2770 6229 Email: cross@crosshk.com

INDIA: Crystal Communications, 10-3-18/4/1, East Marredpalli, Secunderabad – 500026, Andhra Pradesh. Tel/Fax: (040) 27737145 Email: crystal_edwj@rediffmail.com

KENYA: Keswick Books and Gifts Ltd, PO Box 10242-00400, Nairobi.
Tel: (020) 2226047/312639 Email: sales.keswick@africaonline.co.ke

MALAYSIA: Canaanland, No. 25 Jalan PJU 1A/41B, NZX Commercial Centre, Ara Jaya, 47301 Petaling Jaya, Selangor. Tel: (03) 7885 0540/1/2 Fax: (03) 7885 0545 Email: info@canaanland.com.my

Salvation Publishing & Distribution Sdn Bhd, 23 Jalan SS 2/64, 47300 Petaling Jaya, Selangor.
Tel: (03) 78766411/78766797 Fax: (03) 78757066/78756360 Email: info@salvationbookcentre.com

NEW ZEALAND: KI Entertainment, Unit 21 317-321 Woodpark Road, Smithfield, New South Wales 2164, Australia. Tel: 0 800 850 777 Fax: +612 9604 3699 Email: sales@kientertainment.com.au

NIGERIA: FBFM, Helen Baugh House, 96 St Finbarr's College Road, Akoka, Lagos.
Tel: (01) 7747429/4700218/825775/827264 Email: fbfm_1@yahoo.com

PHILIPPINES: OMF Literature Inc, 776 Boni Avenue, Mandaluyong City.
Tel: (02) 531 2183 Fax: (02) 531 1960 Email: gloadlaon@omflit.com

SINGAPORE: Alby Commercial Enterprises Pte Ltd, 95 Kallang Avenue #04-00, AIS Industrial Building, 339420. Tel: (65) 629 27238 Fax: (65) 629 27235 Email: marketing@alby.com.sg

SOUTH AFRICA: Struik Christian Media, 1st Floor, Wembley Square II, Solan Street, Gardens, Cape Town 8001. Tel: +27 (0) 23 460 5400 Fax: +27 (0) 21 461 7662 Email: info@struikchristianmedia.co.za

SRI LANKA: Christombu Publications (Pvt) Ltd, Bartleet House, 65 Braybrooke Place, Colombo 2.
Tel: (9411) 2421073/2447365 Email: christombupublications@gmail.com

USA: David C Cook Distribution Canada, PO Box 98, 55 Woodslee Avenue, Paris, Ontario N3L 3E5, Canada. Tel: 1800 263 2664 Email: sandi.swanson@davidccook.com

CWR is a Registered Charity - Number 294387
CWR is a Limited Company registered in England - Registration Number 1990308

ourses and seminars

ublishing and new media

onference facilities

Transforming lives

CWR's vision is to enable people to experience personal transformation through applying God's Word to their lives and relationships.

Our Bible-based training and resources help people around the world to:
- Grow in their walk with God
- Understand and apply Scripture to their lives
- Resource themselves and their church
- Develop pastoral care and counselling skills
- Train for leadership
- Strengthen relationships, marriage and family life and much more.

Our insightful writers provide daily Bible-reading notes and other resources for all ages, and our experienced course designers and presenters have gained an international reputation for excellence and effectiveness.

CWR's Training and Conference Centres in Surrey and East Sussex, England, provide excellent facilities in idyllic settings – ideal for both learning and spiritual refreshment.

WR Applying God's Word
to everyday life and relationships

R, Waverley Abbey House,
verley Lane, Farnham,
rrey GU9 8EP, UK

ephone: **+44 (0)1252 784700**
ail: **info@cwr.org.uk**
bsite: **www.cwr.org.uk**

gistered Charity No 294387
mpany Registration No 1990308

Dramatic new resource

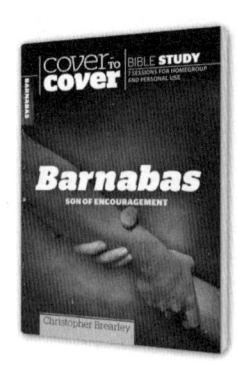

Barnabas – Son of encouragement
by Christopher Brearley

Are we willing to be people like Barnabas, who refuse to give up on others even when they make mistakes? How best can we encourage one another?

72-page booklet, 148x210mm
ISBN: 978-1-85345-911-5

The bestselling *Cover to Cover* Bible Study Series

1 Corinthians
Growing a Spirit-filled church
ISBN: 978-1-85345-374-8

2 Corinthians
Restoring harmony
ISBN: 978-1-85345-551-3

1 Timothy
Healthy churches – effective Christians
ISBN: 978-1-85345-291-8

23rd Psalm
The Lord is my shepherd
ISBN: 978-1-85345-449-3

2 Timothy and Titus
Vital Christianity
ISBN: 978-1-85345-338-0

Acts 1–12
Church on the move
ISBN: 978-1-85345-574-2

Acts 13–28
To the ends of the earth
ISBN: 978-1-85345-592-6

Barnabas
Son of encouragement
ISBN: 978-1-85345-911-5

Ecclesiastes
Hard questions and spiritual answers
ISBN: 978-1-85345-371-7

Elijah
A man and his God
ISBN: 978-1-85345-575-9

Ephesians
Claiming your inheritance
ISBN: 978-1-85345-229-1

Esther
For such a time as this
ISBN: 978-1-85345-511-7

Fruit of the Spirit
Growing more like Jesus
ISBN: 978-1-85345-375-5

Galatians
Freedom in Christ
ISBN: 978-1-85345-648-0

Genesis 1–11
Foundations of reality
ISBN: 978-1-85345-404-2

God's Rescue Plan
Finding God's fingerprints on human history
ISBN: 978-1-85345-294-9

Great Prayers of the Bible
Applying them to our lives today
ISBN: 978-1-85345-253-6

Hebrews
Jesus – simply the best
ISBN: 978-1-85345-337-3

Hosea
The love that never fails
ISBN: 978-1-85345-290-1

Isaiah 1–39
Prophet to the nations
ISBN: 978-1-85345-510-0

Isaiah 40–66
Prophet of restoration
ISBN: 978-1-85345-550-6

James
Faith in action
ISBN: 978-1-85345-293-2

Jeremiah
The passionate prophet
ISBN: 978-1-85345-372-4

John's Gospel
Exploring the seven miraculous signs
ISBN: 978-1-85345-295-6

Joseph
The power of forgiveness and reconciliation
ISBN: 978-1-85345-252-9

Judges 1–8
The spiral of faith
ISBN: 978-1-85345-681-7

Judges 9–21
Learning to live God's way
ISBN: 978-1-85345-910-8

Mark
Life as it is meant to be lived
ISBN: 978-1-85345-233-8

Moses
Face to face with God
ISBN: 978-1-85345-336-6

Names of God
Exploring the depths of God's character
ISBN: 978-1-85345-680-0

Nehemiah
Principles for life
ISBN: 978-1-85345-335-9

Parables
Communicating God on earth
ISBN: 978-1-85345-340-3

Philemon
From slavery to freedom
ISBN: 978-1-85345-453-0

Philippians
Living for the sake of the gospel
ISBN: 978-1-85345-421-9

Prayers of Jesus
Hearing His heartbeat
ISBN: 978-1-85345-647-3

Proverbs
Living a life of wisdom
ISBN: 978-1-85345-373-1

Revelation 1–3
Christ's call to the Church
ISBN: 978-1-85345-461-5

Revelation 4–22
The Lamb wins! Christ's final victory
ISBN: 978-1-85345-411-0

Rivers of Justice
Responding to God's call to righteousness today
ISBN: 978-1-85345-339-7

Ruth
Loving kindness in action
ISBN: 978-1-85345-231-4

The Covenants
God's promises and their relevance today
ISBN: 978-1-85345-255-0

The Divine Blueprint
God's extraordinary power in ordinary lives
ISBN: 978-1-85345-292-5

The Holy Spirit
Understanding and experiencing Him
ISBN: 978-1-85345-254-3

The Image of God
His attributes and character
ISBN: 978-1-85345-228-4

The Kingdom
Studies from Matthew's Gospel
ISBN: 978-1-85345-251-2

The Letter to the Colossians
In Christ alone
ISBN: 978-1-85345-405-9

The Letter to the Romans
Good news for everyone
ISBN: 978-1-85345-250-5

The Lord's Prayer
Praying Jesus' way
ISBN: 978-1-85345-460-8

The Prodigal Son
Amazing grace
ISBN: 978-1-85345-412-7

The Second Coming
Living in the light of Jesus' return
ISBN: 978-1-85345-422-6

The Sermon on the Mount
Life within the new covenant
ISBN: 978-1-85345-370-0

The Tabernacle
Entering into God's presence
ISBN: 978-1-85345-230-7

The Ten Commandments
Living God's Way
ISBN: 978-1-85345-593-3

The Uniqueness of our Faith
What makes Christianity distinctive?
ISBN: 978-1-85345-232-1

For current prices or to order visit www.cwr.org.uk/store
Available online or from Christian bookshops.

Cover to Cover Every Day
Gain deeper knowledge of the Bible

Each issue of these bimonthly daily Bible-reading notes gives you insightful commentary on a book of the Old and New Testaments with reflections on a psalm each weekend by Philip Greenslade.

Enjoy contributions from two well-known authors every two months, and over a five-year period you will be taken through the entire Bible.

Only £2.95 each (plus p&p)
£15.95 for UK annual subscription (bimonthly, p&p included)
£14.25 for annual email subscription
(available from www.cwr.org.uk/store)

Individual issues available in epub/Kindle formats

Prices correct at time of printing

Cover to Cover Complete – NIV Edition
Read through the Bible chronologically

Take an exciting, year-long journey through the Bible, following events as they happened.

- See God's strategic plan of redemption unfold across the centuries
- Increase your confidence in the Bible as God's inspired message
- Come to know your heavenly Father in a deeper way

The full text of the NIV provides an exhilarating reading experience and is augmented by our beautiful:

- Illustrations
- Maps
- Charts
- Diagrams
- Timeline

And key Scripture verses and devotional thoughts make each day's reading more meaningful.

ISBN: 978-1-85345-804-0

For current price or to order visit www.cwr.org.uk/store
Available online or from Christian bookshops.